ARRIVAL PRESS

WINDOWS OF THE SOUL

Edited by

TIM SHARP

First published in Great Britain in 1997 by
ARRIVAL PRESS
1-2 Wainman Road, Woodston,
Peterborough, PE2 7BU
Telephone (01733) 230762

HB ISBN 1 85786 503 0
SB ISBN 1 85786 597 9

FOREWORD

The poets that are included in this anthology come from all walks of life; housewives and lawyers sit alongside police officers and bricklayers. Whether you enjoy reading romantic poetry, or about the horrors of war, or the different people in the world, this is a book you will enjoy reading time and time again.

The poems that I have chosen cover all these subjects and more.

I do hope you enjoy reading this book as much as I did whilst editing it.

Tim Sharp
Editor

CONTENTS

GOOD NIGHT AND GOD BLESS

I think of you my darling as I climb into bed
How I miss you beside me these lonely nights
No strong arms to hold me
No warm breath on my face
No one to take me through the night
To tell me they love me and hold me tight

I wonder if you think of me
As you climb into your bed
In the middle of the North Sea
When the night is dead
And you're alone just like me
Do you wish me there to hold *you* tenderly

To all brave men working weeks away
A few words from your loved ones I will say
God speed and God bless you all out there
Every night we whisper a little prayer
To bring you back safely with your special charms
So again we can hold you close in our arms

I'm a richer person when you are near
Because my darling you are so dear
No diamonds or pearls can comfort me
For in my dreams you are all I see
So before you awake, rise and dress
Remember *I love you good night and God bless*

Angie Simpkin

A SMILE

A smile can lift a dreary day
When clouds are dark and grey.
Happy thoughts can come to mind
Pushing your cares far behind.

The world is not a gloomy place
As clouds will all pass by.
Your day will seem so much brighter
All troubles a little lighter.

Strangers welcome a smile from you
Lifting a frown facing the day anew.
Babies without a worry to their name
Love sharing a smile or playing a game.

Awaking to days with skies of blue
Refreshed and ready to see things through
No matter what the day will bring
Give a smile and your heart will sing.

Ivy E Baker

MESSAGE OF HOPE

If everyone just gave their hearts to Jesus
There'd be no need for counsellors and such,
No need to seek for solace in drug taking,
Searching for ways to find a healing touch.

If everyone acknowledged there's a purpose
Behind the trials we meet with every day,
All leading to a tapestry of glory,
Emblems of beauty gathered on the way.

No need for grieving hearts to break with sorrow,
Despairing souls to sink beneath the pain,
Someone is near to see you through tomorrow,
Strength will be given, and hope be yours again.

Ethel Rayment

THE ULTIMATE SCAPEGOAT

When things go wrong and life is bleak,
We look for someone we can blame.
If then a scapegoat's all we seek,
We call on God and smear his name.

Later, we are sad and chastened;
Remorse and self-reproach abound.
We think our own damnation's hastened;
That no salvation can be found.

Oh, how we underestimate our Saviour.
With endless love that never fails,
Forgiving all our bad behaviour,
He sets us back upon the rails.

And if we should repeat the error
He'll still be there to put us right.
That He may leave us, have no terror,
He'll always lead us to the light.

Francis Marshall

GOTHIC CHRISTMAS

Miss Gentle woke on Christmas Day,
She wandered in her mind
Then plunged into the emptiness
That love had left behind.
Miss Capable awoke,
She nudged her frail friend,
Rubbed shadowed eyes and spoke,
'Get up now Gentle, enjoy the day,
Let's start to cook the lunch,
Aunt Condor's on her way.
If everything's not up to scratch
She's sure to have her say.'
(Miss Capable was quite strong
Her body taught and lean,
She held herself together well.
Life's tutors had been mean.)

Gentle cried amongst the onions,
Capable cursed the sprouts.
Potatoes boiled over,
The turkey lost its clout.
Gentle drinking trifle sherry
Began to fall about.

Aunt Condor settled in her seat,
Her eyes as black as slates
Looked on the crumpled table-cloth
Scattered knives and forks and plates.
She pecked upon the turkey
And spat the trifle out.
She said how peaky Gentle looked,
What was it all about?
So Gentle spoke of cheats and lies,
Told how she'd been betrayed.
She sobbed and revealed all
With deep heart rending sighs.

Aunt Condor fetched her great black bag
And groped with ancient hands,
At length pulled forth a wad
Wrapped in elastic bands.
'The answer to your problem dear,
Time out in far off lands.
The world is spread with pastures new,
With sun and sea and sands.
And so, for now, I'll say Adieu.
Happy New Year, my dear.'

Miss Gentle clapped her hands in glee.
Miss Capable looked slick.
'Tomorrow we'll book the passage,
Get out of here and quick.
Bring more sherry, turn up the sound.
Let's toast the New Year, Gentle
Life's dealt a brand new hand!'

Helena Ball

NINETIES SALESMAN

A mobile bleeps on London's train
Stirring the lady in seat twenty three,
And the suited man keys data into
The lap top on his knee.

A shiny screen glows blue,
A world quivers under fingertips;
Narrowed eyes drink information,
Orders are barked from tight, thin lips.

Targets, figures, margin, profit
Tumble into Orange networks:
Entertainment expenses explored
Benefits, salaries, corporate perks.

Frenetic, pressured business life
Upbeats the order chase
But the merry-go-round cannot hide
Disappointment in his child's face.

And so the professional juggler
Takes another call on the six thirty train
On and on, oblivious to who
One day will take the strain.

Katie Hart

GOD'S PEACE

Lord, when life's busy race
Causes me discontent,
Let me learn, whatever my state,
In You to be content.

Not for diamonds, fur, or gold,
But the peace of God,
In my heart to hold,
Like a deer in the woods, with soft, shy gaze.
Or golden leaves,
On crisp autumn days.

A crystal drop of morning dew,
On a blade of grass,
Or a morning, new.
The sweet smell of earth after pouring rain,
And fragrant, velvet-petalled roses too.

These things are free,
For you and me,
If only we'd remember,
To give our heartfelt thanks to God,
All glory to Him render.

Ann Morton

THE FOUR WINDS

Blow strong wind from the west,
       West wind of love!
Bring your warm showers to me;
       Hot southerly breeze,
       Tenderly play on me.
Breathe your passionate breath on me,
       Wind of the south!
       Blow cold north wind,
       Winter of love,
       Come to me,
       I shall not scorn thee!
You bring the warm blanket of snow
To cover my naked form, hidden beneath
       Is spring newly born!
Blow east wind,
You cannot penetrate;
For love like a green velvet mantle,
       Keeps me warm!

Patricia Arnett

HE'S IN HIS 80'S

He lives alone, with fourteen steps to climb
Up to his flat, and after taking bus to town
And calling in essential shops, in time
To catch returning bus. Nice to sit down.
Then up again and carrying bags to flat,
And up those steps again, one at a time
Switch on fire, unpack bags, remembering that
Enjoyment of the walk, when in one's prime,
Before arthritis struck. How rich the feel
Of movement, now no longer here with him.
He has his books, paints, his scribbles to deal
With time, pity poverty makes things so grim.
Though come to that there must be many more
People as ill and equally as poor.

Richard Saunders

AUTUMN TIDE

For those now reaching their autumn years
Take heart as this *golden* time appears
Things don't always look fair, truth be told
If all life's about is getting old
So much inclined, when strength's diminished
To feel, at times, we're all but finished
Difficult to take as ageing slows
When *get up and go* gets up and goes
Hark! When outer vigour starts to wane
Chance for spiritual power to reign
This period is providential
Begging the question: What's essential?

There comes to us all, in time, a need
To journey forth at moderate speed
Because the outer body's slowing
Need not proclaim the end of growing
Different now from the quest of youth
Yet never too late to seek for truth
This era can herald a new start
Learning what's buried in your own heart
Like the pearl hidden in oyster's trap
Within you hides knowledge you can tap
Daily relaxing meditation
Can be a boon for revelation

No amount of wishful *if only*
Changes one atom what has to be
It would be a shame, having long toiled
To allow days ahead to be spoiled
So do your best to let worry cease
Then autumn tide will bring inner peace

Tina Lipman

JUNE 25TH 1994

Such memories the Nineties bring,
And when I'm old and grey,
I'll remember most of all,
My daughter's wedding day.

There she stood in satin dress,
I watched the people stare,
Such a lovely sight to see,
So proud I was of Claire.

My mind it drifted back so far,
To nineteen seventy three,
To the twelfth, the second month,
The day she came to me.

Those memories of years gone by,
Were more than I could bear,
Her loving smile, her tender kiss,
Blue eyes and auburn hair.

Every time I washed her hair,
I waited for the cries,
'Daddy! Where's the flannel!
The soap's gone in my eyes.'

If I could only have her back,
To have those years long gone,
To wipe her tears, to hear her cry,
'I want a plaster on.'

But I have to look ahead,
I must forget the pain,
Perhaps one day she'll have a Claire,
To bring me joy again.

John Napier Williams

THE LETTER

Upon this pebbled way we walked
Moon magnified above the mist
In evening's chill we softly talked
And then inevitably kissed.

The Severn rippled on its way
Caressing banks of willow trees
Where water fowl in reed beds lay
And Gloucester bells hung on the breeze.

A scented letter you did send
With teardrops, briefly wrote farewell
To offer friendship to the end
So lost its vaguely perfumed smell.

Best not to think, as I now walk
The gently lapping river shore
Of days when I would lay and gaze
Upon those eyes I did adore.

Clive W Macdonald

DIVIDED COUNTRY
(In memory of Katrina Rennie and Eileen Duffy)

Blue angel eyes, blue angel eyes.
Now your body in blood still lies.
In this province of bullet and gun.
People are dying one by one.
Katrina, Eileen, they are but two.
Were killed for what? Oh why? By who?
Young innocents still in teenage years.
Who didn't realise their hopes and fears.
At the graveside their families weep.
As candles in silent vigil keep.
Fathers, brothers, and sons have died.
In this country of great divide.
Now the flowers of youth have departed.
Leaving loved ones broken hearted.
Churchmen wring their hands in despair.
At the two bodies lying there,
But tears will not bring back, ones so sweet.
As two angels their maker meet.
The men that hide behind the gun.
What do they think that they have won.
Peace will not come to green fields
Till the gunman and bomber yield.

Jim Dolbear

HOW CAME THE FLOWERS?

Rose watered sun light
       danced, on medieval glass,
day-star's dust hung still,
       caught within time's gilded web
fingers, dank and chill,
       rose, creeping cold; stepping from
the sunbeam came a
       band of spectres, laughing souls,
no heads 'neath arms nor
       shrieking ghouls, but merry folk
enticing me to
       join the dance; a slight wraith now
wavers by, she holds
       fair meadow-sweet, and golden
hair with daisies bound;
       smiling, she extends her hand
in friendly gesture,
       fingers touch - but I recoil!
For she was of a
       deathly cold; I woke to find
the sun now chill, and
       O! there lay on my iced hand
gentle meadow-sweet, and
       daisies chained by golden hair,
blushed, by rose - pale light.

Was she true wraith petal-decked?
If not, how come the flowers?

Teresa Jeanne Smith

THE LADIES IN BLACK

Shivering in the morning air,
the widow shops with studied care,
purse pressed to her dingy weeds,
its plight must match her every need,
a frugal content she will heed,
and a plan her meagre fare.

Serene of face and calm of eye,
oblivious of the noonday sky,
deaf to a city symphony,
intent on blessed sanctuary,
each sister clasps her rosary,
swiftly rustling by.

Shadows flit where a moon beams down,
on tightened skirt and skimpy gown,
the trap is set for human prey,
clad in slinky dark array,
gliding through the alleyways,
go ladies of the town.

Ivy Wood

FROM WANDERING

In a circle its wondrous peace
Touched with a certain silver light
That neither noontide make star shine;
Or glow the things I have prayed
In the golden musky aftertime of love.

For a little while we stopped this spinning world
In the longing words of relief,
And in mind give me your lips of love
And I will breathe a dream into your heart,
Blessings you in mind as a firm of affection.

In the first kind finds more delight
So be patient believe these blessings,
I greet you with praise and thanksgiving
And may unfold your dream to guide you through the day
When the passion of love and blessings are revealed in reason.

Heather Aspinall

THE WONDER OF GOD

The Lord moves in mysterious ways
His wonders to bestow
Yes we've heard this many times
But do we really know
Why so much happens to us
To make our awareness grow
He gives us our gifts of mind
And our eyes to see
So why oh why are some of us blind
And why can't we *all* be free
So many things are never clear
To us on this earthly land
I'm sure before we all pass on
He'll help us understand
Some are here for many years
And we need to learn so much
But some are taken back so soon
Why shouldn't it be such?
Perhaps we're meant to wonder
At all His mystery
His gift could be the knowledge
That our loved ones we will see
But while we're here let's enjoy
His beauty of life all around
Touch the flowers and the trees
In streams hear nature's sound
Know these are His gifts to us
When tranquility you have found.

Moira Michie

LIFE AFTER DIVORCE

Wear a smile, never a frown,
Don't let the whole thing get you down
The sun will shine again, never fear,
As you put your best foot forward
                for another year.

It's easy to regret, take more than
                your share of the blame,
But these things might have happened
                all the same.
Who knows what makes a marriage die,
Was it a bad patch, or all a lie.

Don't spend your life in bitterness,
Hate will only swallow you up.
Fill your life with thoughts of other things,
Live life to the full, and you'll soon be
                on the way up.

Remember, you are a special person,
And confidence will return.
Show the world you mean business,
And never give way to a frown.

Anne Roberts

TEN BROOKSIDE

Number ten is my house and home where I reside,
By a brook and a garden, I tend with pride.

Sixteen brick houses stand in a row,
And I have seen many neighbours come and go,
Still I remain at ten Brookside,
Until no longer I'll survive.

There are babies I have known,
To adults they have grown,
And some that have married,
Now have babies of their own.
Others have divorced and moved away,
Hoping to find love and happiness another day.

There have been Harrises, Burtons, Jacksons and Palmers
Some were forest workers, coalmen and farmers;
There were also Richardsons, Blacketts, Harding and Hood,
Most were good neighbours and some not so good.

Smiths , Aldouses, Duells and Ives,
And many incidents happened that caused surprise;
But never a dull moment as days went by,
Without making chatter for the Brookside wives.

For more than forty years there has been,
Memories of happiness and sadness I have seen,
Some of us have grown old and many have died.

But that is life, like the returning tide,
People will come and go and still reside
By the brook in the country,
At ten Brookside.

G S H Seymour

PILGRIMAGE

To the strains, of anchors away.
Our liner, slowly glided on its way
Starting our trip, to the Holy Land.
We are sailing, played the band.

Calling at different ports on the way.
Until at last, came the big day
Sailing into Haifa, to disembark
Eager for our Jerusalem, visit to start.

Our first sight of it, we'll never forget
Our feelings so mixed, at the sight of it.
This Holy Land, spread before our eyes
On this crisp March morning, under blue skies.

The dome of the rock, glistening under the sun
Brought forth gasps of wonder from everyone,
To walk along the same route, as Jesus carried the cross
Seeing the other pilgrims, on the same, journey as us.

On to the Mount of Olives,
To walk in the Garden of Gethsemane.
The rows upon rows, of olive trees,
In perfect symmetry.

The trip on the Sea of Galilee
Then on to Bethlehem, Jesus' birth place to see.
On to see the River Jordan, The Wailing Wall.
So much to see, no time left at all.

Now for our trip back home, to start.
With a feeling of gladness in our hearts.
Filled with memories, to treasure forever.
To bring out and savour, at our leisure.

Enid Grace

DEPARTING

You turn and are gone
  life stops
Come back come back
  I shout in silence though
  the uproar of my grief
But you are deaf and
  I am dying
  dying
  for you have cremated me.
O lover,
  scatter me across the hills
  and let the fragments fall
  where the wind stops
  against a dark stone wall
  and I will cry no more
O lover,
  only the earth will shudder now
  as a last tormented sigh
  is slowly torn from
  this lover's cry
Goodbye my love,
  Goodbye

Elizabeth Berns

THE YEAR TOMORROW YIELDS

Pilgrim, see the land ahead,
Land you'll enter and possess.
Not the desert where you've been,
With its barren loneliness.

Not the clouds of sand and dust,
Not the trackless, howling waste;
Not the plains of yesteryear,
Nor those drifting dunes you've paced.

See the view that lies before,
'Tis a land of hills and vales.
Watered rich by heavenly rain,
Where the Lord's care never fails.

'Tis the year tomorrow yields,
To God's loved ones who obey.
Going on beneath His gaze,
To the land called Promised Day.

Ken Millar

THE CROSS UPON MY HEART

The sweet scent of white roses whispered over my stilled grave
Filtering their comfort over the cross upon my heart that laid.
Those full bearing petals caressed all around moist earth
When a sudden breeze had come from a heaven mingled in mirth.

An angel so splendour and fair came as she glowed with a gleam
And carried me upon a journey into a world I had not seen.
For a short time I travelled freely like a floating cloud.
Higher, and higher I had risen in my flowing silky shroud.

It was then that my lighted eyes fell upon his adoring face
In the garden which was entwined and woven like softly lace.
Ah! heaven such a wondrous and miracled place of things
Where saints so majestic, and courteous dance as they sing.

My Lord had stood before me with a calmly and kindly smile
Reaching out for me with his paled hand that felt so fragile.
Side by side we walked through the kingdom of his reign
Where I would no more feel the suffering of any pain.

He turned to me as he held the cross and said
'Do not be afraid of me now that you have been shown the way
For this is my heaven of peace where you shall eternally stay.'
And with observed eyes, and holding the cross, I knelt down to pray
For I know that to roam the heaven I need not ever become afraid.

Amanda Jane Martin

THE GIFTS

The good Lord could have made this world in black and white,
So we could tell the difference 'twixt day and night.

But then we'd have no sunrise rays of opal, green and gold,
Nor yet the flaming sunset blaze when scarlet clouds unfold

And show a path of glory which leads up to the sun,
Throbbing brighter and yet brighter, until the day is done.

Pale, creamy-yellow primroses, with leaves of gentle green;
Flamboyant golden buttercups - the brightest flowers I've seen.

White roses? Yes, of course there are, and every other hue, -
Shell-pink, salmon, vivid reds . . . and even some of blue.

Our dear Lord could have kept the colours; He didn't have to share,
And then we'd have had just black and white, but no - His unbounded care

For those He made and loves so dear means He wants the best for us:
He shared the colours and the beauty with never any fuss.

'That which I know is beautiful I'll share with everyone,
But the brightest gift I have to give is My own beloved Son.'

Marjorie Piggins

TIME FOR LOVE

As the year does fly on by
I feel on such an incredible high
Only you could take me much higher
and that's the one thing I now desire
Time is of the essence
for I need and crave your presence
especially now my dove
as you have openly confessed your love
I can think of nothing but the time
that we should be spending together
of every passing moment that could be
filled with unabated passion and pleasure
So let the world race on by
and come to me your ever loving guy
and let us live our lives
at our sweet leisure.

Phil Dee

EVENSONG

We see before us the end of an era,
As the twentieth century draws to a close,
And we hear in its last elegiac song,
The echoing note that is bellicose.

Anger surrounds us like a shroud,
Restricting generosity,
Instead, it's every man for himself,
Resulting in ferocity.

Our government and rule of law
Are discredited and held in contempt;
The victims pay for the guilty ones,
Whilst the hardened criminals are exempt.

We've lost all stability,
Jobs and homes are no longer secure;
You're over the top at thirty five,
And then you're the object of cynosure.

We address each stranger by Christian name
To prove we're politically correct,
But a neighbour can live in poverty
And die alone of social neglect.

Human dignity's been sacrificed
To lip service and hypocrisy,
This is the hallmark of the nineties -
An ersatz democracy!

B Gordon

THAT'S HOW IT WAS IN THE FORTIES

An old brick building dimly lit, with cobwebs everywhere,
A hovel to the fenmen, and their tools were stored in there,
Built on the end of the farmhouse, had a two piece wooden door,
A single window at one end, and granite blocks for a floor.

The fenman were a thrifty breed, not known to throw much away,
They hung everything in the hovel, for it may be of use some day,
Old horse shoes adorn the walls, bits of chain hang down from nails,
Even though the cows have gone, they have kept the milking pails.

All the tools have their place, either on or under the bench,
They never talk of spanners, to the fenmen they're a wrench,
Above the bench were many shelves, full, each and every one,
With a special place for the oil can, and of course the old grease gun.

In the middle of the floor, on a block the anvil stands,
There's a furnace and the hammers, used by these craftsmen's hands,
Implements of any age, were repaired here in the den,
They had to be kept in order, ready to work out in the fen.

There were many visitors to the hovel, including livestock from
                                                the farm,
Some found it much more homely, than the big old wooden barn,
The cats slept in the corner, in the comfort of an old armchair,
Until the rooster in the rafters, crowed loud into the morning air.

The rooster was the fenman's clock, reliable and never late,
Soon the farmhouse breakfast would be on each fenman's plate,
The animals were next to feed, food was served in all the pens,
And then the fenmen set to work, among the treasures in their dens.

Those olden days were the best, fields surrounded with hedges
                                                so green,
And horses out numbered tractors, hence the air was fresh and clean,
This was the nineteen forties, there was peace throughout the land,
No drugs or any violent crime, in fact a time when life was
                                                really grand.

R A Wenn

LOVE IS A RADIANT CLOUD

Love is a radiant cloud
Silvering the ocean proud
Wherein drowned suns appear
Ablaze in the twilight sere
Without a sound.

Praise, praise be to God,
I risen above a clod,
Unworthy every way,
Yet I marvel His day
As rivers flood.

What care in the world
Where cruel hours whirl,
Faith, hope, joy away?
Will I then not kneel or pray
Feeling His love unfurl?

For each hour revelation,
Prayer, thought, elation,
A song light angels send
Without music, without end,
God's re-creation.

O let His poet sing,
Bright lyrist on the wing
Of love, O radiant cloud,
Hidden in what is found,
A mystic thing.

Deny love and the light
Perishes from my sight.
O universe I bless
The silent loneliness
Of God's love tonight.

Christopher Dickinson

WHERE ARE YOU NOW

Jesus came to teach us love.
So we, when young, we told.
Came long ago and far away
In the Bible stories of old.

But today! Where is he when needed
In this world of war and strife.
Where brother fights against brother.
And a man might slay his wife.

Now is when we need the love.
He came to show us how.
We need the joy and laughter.
We need it here and now.

Tammy Benham

A SUMMER EVENING

Into the stillness of a summer evening, the blackbird poured his song.
A symphony of liquid music spilled into the air, and all along
The riverbank came answering the rise and fall
Of other bird song sweetly echoing the blackbird's call.

Through the trees the sun's last rays reached out across the sky,
Fluffy clouds changed colour and entranced the eye.
I stood transfixed by radiant beauty spread for all to see,
My spirits soared, my soul responded to the vision shown to me.

And as I walked along beside a garden wall,
The scent of honeysuckle, sweetest smell of all,
Mingled with night-scented stocks and fragrant rose, my senses filling,
Causing my joyful heart to overflow once more with thanksgiving.

All this given freely for anyone to take and hold,
To keep within the inner mind, to fold
Into a precious store, to recollect and to remember once again,
When winter days are here and only memories of summertime remain.

Linda Leach

THE COMPETITION

On to the ice the skaters come,
Their silver blades a-swishing,
To gain the highest marks there are,
That's what they all are wishing.

The youngsters all are quiet and still,
Their eager hearts are pumping,
While round the hall their friends go mad,
You hear their feet a-thumping.

The twirls, the jumps, the triple loops,
Are done to near perfection,
And as their hours of practice shows,
Mums gaze on with affection.

The music flows around the hall,
Some quick, and some much slower,
The jumps go high into the air,
Then change, to sway much lower.

The costumes that the skaters wear,
Gleam and shimmer in the lights,
Which dance and flicker round the hall,
And make such wonderful sights.

And so the competition ends,
As winners hold their medals high,
The losers vow to practice more,
On that you can rely.

Isobel Crumley

RICHARD'S CHRISTMAS

C hristmas Day is
H ere!
R ichard awakes at 4am
I t's time to open our
S acks, is
T he cry!
M inutes later
A ll presents are tried out
S weets eaten by the box full.
  - CDs played and new computer
D isks loaded in!
A ll by 6am
Y es, Christmas Day is here!

I feel really
S ick, comes the next cry!

H ave a lie down dear,
E laine replies - she
  knows *her*
R ichard - is the best
  . . .husband
E ver!

E Duggan

WHEN YOU WENT AWAY

When you went away
My world did too,
I was no longer *us*
Now a who.
The oceans left
And a puddle appeared,
The colours vanished
And blackness smeared.
The forests were cut
And woods were cleared,
The branches became twigs
But then they disappeared.
The animals went
Both common and rare,
You're not here with me
So I don't care.
Will this grieving
Never end
Without your loving arms
To lend
Or your lips
Which used to tend
Without your kisses
To comfort me
And now only a picture
For me to see.

Natalie Bennett

PATHWAY TO HEAVEN

Lord help us each day
to follow your way.
To listen to you
and not to ourselves.
Lord help us to teach
others the way,
of following you
the only true way.

Anna King

EASTER THOUGHTS

He came, He went,
He was Heaven sent.

On the cross he died,
for you and for me,
time stood still,
and then the dawn,
when all did mourn.
A miracle begun many years before,
with a lot more in store.

On the third day,
He rose from the dead,
and left his earthly bed,
from the womb
to the tomb,
no ordinary life lost,
and at what cost?

He stretched out his hand
and touched the sand,
all who walk here,
need never fear,
for now He is risen
from this earthly prison.

And those who follow,
be it today or tomorrow,
will always know
that He loved them so.

David Carress

PREPARATIONS

I've sent the very last *Thank you* note
and a New Year card or two,
and now I'm trying to tell myself
that there's nothing left to do.

The cards and the decorations
were packed up by Twelfth Night;
I've brought my gift-list up to date
so I know that that's all right.

I've put up my new calendars,
started the diary too;
I've entered all the details
we need to carry through,

transferred important birthdays
from ninety-four to five,
and wondered what next year will bring
and if I'll be alive!

But while I am, there certainly
is one more thing to do:
ask the Giver of all gifts
for guidance firm and true.

Geraldine Squires

IT IS JANUARY

And the scars and wounds
Of the Old Year's dying and the New Year's birth
Are wrapped in a bandage of snow.

So, I can see fox prints leading to my frozen pond
And remember how only yesterday I met her
By the closed church door; paw lifted from a wound sustained
Traversing the harsh man's landscape; walking
Clumsily, like two children bound in a three legged race,
Searching scraps to subsidise her limited menu.

Yes now, by my frozen pond I see her fox prints; three,
Not four, one far deeper than the other two
Where she leaned heavily on her less supported side,
Recall the pain reflected in her eyes as she stared,
Surprised into mine, sensing sympathy, and almost smiled.

I see the indentation in the snow on the icy pond
Where her nose pressed to dip dry tongue into her own reflection,
Meeting only refrigeration, rigid, resisting her frozen fur muzzle.
Her disappointed fox prints limp away down the winterland garden,
Under the wire fence into her wooded world,
To while away pain and thirst and the night in dark lair
Until morning might bring her lucky relief with a thaw.

And I remember how cosily in the night I was curled
Under eider duck duvet; warmed through by hot dinner,
Chocolates and mulled wine from a bountiful cupboard,
Not one which is almost bare.

So as I stare this morning at her fox prints in the powdery snow,
I resolve to share the scraps from my plate
Too generously endowed; she shall have her fill,
And the ice on the frozen pond will be broken;
Her thirst shall be quenched.

Christine Barham

THE FINAL FAREWELL

The day we dread came finally,
bringing home the death as reality.
The final farewell to our loved one.

The future seems hard to exist - without you,
plans must be made, arrangements finalised.
Coming to realise you're no longer here.

Death makes me realise how short life is,
how quickly it could happen,
how unfair it seems,
to those left behind.

Decisions that are out of our control,
confuse, worry and mystify.
God's decision is final,
yet seems so unfair.
Comforting cards and unification of families,
reassuring thoughts help me through.
Earth is hell and damn hard work,
the dead will be better off in another world - Heaven,
a place untouchable to evil.
Where their life goes on with others,
waiting until our day comes,
where we will be re-united - as one.

Helen Rees-Smith

THE MIRROR

The Romans had mirrors of burnished metal
But the reflection was not clear.
Today for mirrors of glass we settle
And at our reflection we peer.

We see a face and say 'That's me'
The image now is clearer.
But others beneath the surface see
And come to know us better.

There is One who looks more deep
And sees within our hearts
The secrets that we seek to keep
The sin that we hold fast.

And yet our God will love us still
And seek a change within.
With His Spirit He will fill,
And free us from all sin.

Peggy Leech

CREATION'S GRACE

A panoramic view stretched before us
Quilted like patchwork, revealing
Colours, rich in splendour,
Boundaries, blankets of green.

High on horizon, Crowborough Beacon,
Bearing right, Cross in Hand,
Sweeping left, Burgess Hill,
Far distant appears North Downs.

Pathways visible across the fields,
Inviting leisurely walks,
Smoke ascending, busy farmers
Clearing, cutting, preparing.

Trees nestling around small holdings,
Sheltering, protecting, concealing.
Horses gallop, around their paddock,
Cattle grazing, mellow, content.

Shadows casting light, then dark,
Enhancing the Downs with charm,
Rolls of straw, crops of corn,
Fields of golden, a wondrous sight.

Pride filled our being
With the scene we observed
Feeling contentment knowing
Nature's gift was all one desired.

Lorna Tippett

NEW YEAR

We've torn down the tinsel and the cards
From people who we hardly ever see.
The family have gone back to work and school,
The sudden silence paralyses me.
I'm left to face your death and all it means,
The endless years I'll never see your face.
I miss your humour and your big brown eyes,
Your breezy optimism and your grace.
We are confronted with our half-beliefs,
With truths that we would rather do without,
I could really use your quiet good sense,
Your practicality, your lack of doubt.
I've carefully labelled all your photographs,
I nurse my horror and my lonely rage,
I want to see you smiling in the flesh
And not just from the icy album page.
I miss your phone calls, miss your funny charm,
I'm just a robot filled with silent screams,
But late at night as snowfall coats the town
We talk and laugh in vivid life-like dreams.
Now with my son you stand so far removed,
Both wrecked upon a distant nameless shore,
Without my anchors I am cast adrift,
My guiding stars snuffed out for evermore.
You touched the waxy berries on my tree
And said this winter would be hard and long.
Did you know you wouldn't see the spring?
The tree still stands forlorn and you are gone.
Your worn gold ring sits on my finger now,
From your cold flesh to mine it passed in hours.
I'll feel your healing touch in spring's rebirth,
In the unfolding trees and tender flowers.

Judy Pavier Wilson

YE HAVE DONE IT UNTO ME

I was lonely, did you visit me?
I was sick but did you care?
I was blinded, did you help me see?
I was ladened, did you share?

I was frightened, did you strengthen me?
I was lost but did you show?
I was begging, did you heed my plea?
I was weeping, did you know?

I was helpless, did you support me?
I was tired but did you cheer?
I was care-bound, did you comfort me?
I was Jesus, were you there?

Pam Baker

A FRESH START

New experiences beckon, like neon lights in the city sky
Eerily leading me on, forcing me to make decisions
Will I be successful, will I fail? Perhaps, to both

Last look back over my shoulder at what was the old
Eagerly looking forward to what will become the new
Anxious but optimistic that the right choice has been made
Vestige of reality put behind me for a while
Escaping into new dreams, new hopes and aspirations
So vital to the open mind of constant learning

Roseanna May

NORTHERN IRELAND

A British soldier on patrol in a Northern Ireland town
His senses are alert to the tiniest sound
As darkness surrounds him, he's not by himself
There's a patrol of his mates, if he needs any help
He slowly walks through the streets, always his back to the wall
For the bombers this night are having a ball
Bomb blasts are everywhere, quite near they sound
There's an explosion to his left, so he drops to the ground
Luckily for him, because where he would have stood
An ugly piece of shrapnel was embedded in some wood
It's soon time for the patrol, to return to their camp
There's sweat in their foreheads their bodies feel damp
As some lay on their beds with cigarette in their hands
Some drinking, some talking, whilst others just stand
Most thinking, we can unwind for a while, and relax for a little
Deep down they know they can't, their nerves are so brittle
But soon their stint is over, across the water they will go
Happy in the knowledge, that the people will all know
Of the courage and guts of the troops over there
For the thankless job they are doing, do you think it's fair?
The cemeteries are full of people who tried to do their best
In this strange hope soon the troubles may soon cease
All pray most sincerely for peace . . . peace . . . peace.

W James

CHURCH

I'm not a disbeliever; I would like to go to church.
Occasionally I venture there, because for truth I search.
I feel I'm pleased to be there, and I think it's going well;
But then I find a part of me is wanting to rebel.

It's happened that so often when I've given it a try,
The sermon's on commitment, and the whole thing goes awry.
I'm open to the teaching, and I wish my thoughts were pure;
But can I be committed when I know I am not sure?

I'm a very patient person, but I have to give an ear
To much that is not new to me - not what I want to hear.
It is aimed at little children or at those who have not thought.
It seems to me a waste of time to sit there learning nought.

And it's when I am so critical, that I begin to hate
Myself for all those nasty thoughts, and I become irate.
And quite often I have found that on the Sundays when I've gone,
The service never seems to stop - it just goes on and on.

To a very ancient church today I went once more to try,
And something seemed to move me here - don't know the reason why.
There was beauty in the language; there was beauty all around;
A stirring of my feelings; which was for me profound.

Toni Backhouse

ANTS

I wish that they would leave me alone
I don't invite them in my home
How they get in, I do not know
I must find out, they've got to go
Here they come, how many more
Blasted things all over the floor
They're in the cupboards, up the wall
First in the kitchen, then the hall
Still they come in, it's unfair odds
How do I get rid of the little sods
Give them Nippon someone said
That's the stuff to *knock 'em dead*
I killed them all, out of the way
Their friends and relations are here today
Oh dear me, I cannot win
These have wings, they just flew in.

Joan Jeffries

JUST MY FEET

My feet are bare,
Sometimes socks I wear,
Sometimes shoes.

My skin is pink,
My toenails white,
My feet are also small.

My feet are flat,
And very thin,
But I skip, hop, jump, and dance,
And keep warm,
Then they become sweaty,
Then I make haste,
And hope for cold weather.

Margaret Roberts

LITTLE ONES

Before you came I was scared
Scared you would not want
To take the place
Of our cat, Sweep.
Whom we had for eleven years
Before going to the angels.
Now
You came
From the animal rescue centre
The two of you
So small
But quick
Wanting to be loved
Sunshine.
Two tiny fragile kittens
Whom we now adore.
They have not taken your place
But have brought
Light
Into the home again.

Pat Jones

CHURCH ON THE GREEN

A stranger passing,
The church on the green
Its bells had a welcoming ring.
The church doors were open wide.
The stranger stopped to listen,
Songs of praise taking place inside,
Good Christian, side by side,
The standing people,
In homage sang,
Out from beneath the steeple,
Voices in common pray,
Soft sweet and serene;
Full of love and care.
Through the open doors,
The stranger did creep,
Into a church he had never been before,
He stood beside and sang,
With that heavenly choir,
An entire congregation turned,
Many faces, the stranger faced.
Many eyes said
Come in welcome friend,
No words need to be said,
Say your grace,
In the church on the green.

B G Clarke

GIVING

Life's good when you are giving,
Look around, offer your love,
Time on earth is for living,
Lift your eyes to God above.

Just spare a thought for others,
There are those who might need us,
Love to sisters and brothers,
Be around, but do not fuss.

To all you pass give a smile,
It can lighten someone's day,
Pause and tarry for a while,
It will send them on their way.

With hope, that life will brighten,
All their sorrows will phase out,
Their days on earth will lighten,
Prayers of thanks to God they shout.

Every hour of every day,
Give love and hope to all,
Live yourself in such a way,
You are at God's beck and call.

Suzanne Joy Golding

TIME

I cannot heal your broken heart
For I do not have the tool
But I will try to play my part
When life has been so cruel

I only wish that I could do more
To make your load a little lighter
But of one thing I am sure
The furture does get brighter

Though I know it does take time
And time goes by so slow
So just take one day at a time
And your confidence will grow

D A White

LIE

A bitter wound struck so deeply
Yet no evidence remained
To a stranger's eye.
The words said so intensely
Had done what they had not aimed
And broken the existing tie.
Taking the life from within me,
Leaving me helpless and unable to respond.
Alone I had not wished to be
As I was left, after the breaking of this everlasting bond.

Ghazala Rashid

BLACKBERRY DAYS

So shall we go a - blackberrying?
Hedgerows beckon, rich with fruit;
The glistening berries, sun-ward turned,
Proclaim a feast of summer's loot.
Across the stubbled fields we'll go
To where the brambles twist and twine,
Purple leaf and purple fruit
With their guardian thorns combine.
Armed with baskets, curving stick,
We see the largest fruit of all
Where tangled thickets clutch and claw,
We stretch, to see the bounty fall!
But slowly, slowly, baskets fill,
Brimming till they take no more;
Fingers stained, hair dishevelled,
Scratches where the brambles tore.
So now with shadows lengthening,
We turn to leave the sunlit field
To other times, another year,
And wait to taste next summer's yield.

Iris Coventry

TO MY FATHER

I watch him die a bit each day
A slow descent to nevermore;
A childlike soul of once what was
A wraith to haunt me evermore.

With roles reversed I tend to him
When once he used to tend to me;
Poor old man so tired of life
I pray he stays a while with me.

At times I wish that he was gone
But still he needs to cling to me;
Mind twists the man back to the child
But Father he will always be . . .

Joanne White

GOD IS MY STRENGTH

God grant me strength, to do thy will
To give love, and receive my fill,
For thou are the master I must obey,
Thou will not forsake me, if I pray

Each little care, I bring to thee
Bowing head, and bended knee.
Forgiveness I ask, for the wrong I have done
Penitent I stand before thee, thou holy one

I am not worthy in thy presence to be
Thy word is my comfort, thy hand guideth me
My path is straight thou lights my way
Each morning, night, and all through the day

Mary Seddon

LAST REUNION

When we, in quick mortality's last act,
into the shadow world of death subside;
when this once animated soul breathes not,
speaks not, sees and hears not; what then
for those whose song is tuned to His command?
And what of those still 'prisoned here on earth?
Cocooned in solitude, their nearest snatched
at times with savage haste; but at the best
eased silently away, whilst they survey
and count the cost of this, a skirmish lost.
Our hope, alas unspoken, as in turn
their shadow creeps, is that they forsake doubt's
fertile soil, and life's last frontier breach,
to join us here, immortal, now in reach.

Philip Dyson

FAITH

Do you have faith on which to lean
Facing tomorrow, and all the unseen,
Can you bear life's heavy load.
Travelling a seemingly endless road?

So many problems we have to face,
Can you meet them with good grace,
Not letting them get you down,
Greeting each day with a smile, not a frown?

Not yielding to temptations that beset your way,
Living a Christian life day by day,
Helping others who are in need,
With a cheery word and kindly deed.

I am sure that God holds the key,
To unfold to us our life's destiny,
If we believe, and our faith is strong,
With him to guide us, we can't go wrong.

So live your faith, from day to day,
Ask for God's help to show you the way,
Then maybe others will follow your lead,
Finding that faith is something *they* need.

E Kathleen Jones

ALL FOR LOVE

I reached out to my daughter in her cot,
Who gurgled, blew bubbles and cried a lot.

I reached out to my son who crawled around,
With sturdy knees upon the ground,

I reached out for the man I called mine,
Who worked for us until his prime.

Our off-springs gathered more,
Booties, shawls, heartaches for sure.

In the family tree hopes grow with trust,
Yet? Somewhere along the way,
In the garden the serpent's at play,
Filling those apples full of holes.

But if those souls we cherish, become cold,
As well they may, as we grow old,
Then I will say on my judgement day,
I did it all for love.

Joan McAvoy

VERTICAL NEW YEAR

New year is now upon us,
It's clear that last year's gone,
New beginnings and promises
Each to start as we mean to go on.
Trying to think of the future,
Everyone still learning from past,
Each new year is a time for beginning
Not just walking the same worn out paths.
Now in time we will see many new years,
I'm sure not all will be as good or as planned,
Now that time always moves on so fast now,
Till new year when time rules the land.
Yet we look on now into this year,
So many people with their own hopes and dreams,
Each expectation so different
Varying greatly between both you and me.
Everyone alert now as the clock hands strike tall
New Year greetings to all

Aleena Matthews

MAKE A DIFFERENCE THIS YEAR

What can I change, take up, give up,
is the cry as the old years fade;
perhaps later on when I've filled my cup
I'll dream an idea to put all in the shade.

We vie with each other as to who can do best,
who promise the most radical change;
we always want to look better than the rest
as the old year and the new year exchange.

Don't we remember what happens each year;
each of us lasts a day or a week,
then promises made over wine glass or beer
fade faster than the blush on our cheek.

And what about those who can't change their life,
those who are desperate, dying or ill,
those who live amongst pain, war and strife,
unable to do much of their own free will.

Maybe when we make our pledges so trite
we should think for a while of others,
those whose year is one long, dark night,
for we are, in the end, all brothers.

So let's try to make a difference this year,
to think, my friends, and think deep,
to all unite to put an end to world fear
and let peace be the pledge that we keep.

Wendy Ray

THE MOURNING DEW

How sad the morning grass all drenched in dew,
The wet droplets afar all about lie
For the night was wept; states its view
'Though we know not for what nor why.

Perhaps the moon hid from the sun
And a sombre darkness saddened the night
Whilst the storm clouds gathered to run
And left it unhappy in lonesome plight.

Perhaps the stars failed to appear;
With heaven gone, the night lost faith so mourned,
Believing the Earth's end needs to be feared
With man's raging ills he has spawned.

Where the night bears witness to death
And, disturbed by the dreadful waste of life,
Thinks to spray the grass with damp breath;
An epitaph to summon a morning fife.

There in the sadness of dew is relief;
To know the dark fears of the night
For the mourning grass, dampened with grief,
Displays this wake as an insight.

Lloyd Carley-West

MY THEORY TEST
(Dedicated to my son Ian Balchin)

I feel so happy.
I feel so great.
The day is lovely.
And the place is great.
The sun is shining.
And the birds are singing.
As if to rejoice this lovely day.

Then came the letter.
It said I am sorry but you have failed.
The sun went in and the clouds came out.
The birds stopped singing.
I feel so down.

Theory - I thought so what.
I am not the only one to fail.
I'll try again, and guess what.
The sun came out once again.

Judith Balchin

MY LORD SUSTAINS ME IN TIMES OF TROUBLE

Though I walk, oftentimes, through the vale of tears,
I know Thou art by my side,
To hold my hand and to calm my fears,
Whatever may betide.

The burden is hard and the journey's long,
Sometimes too hard to bear,
But you fill my heart with some lovely song
And I know that Thou art there.

Oh, don't let me falter on my way,
When I pass through the valley of pain.
Bear me up in Your arms, safe from all alarms,
And keep me in Your narrow way.

How oft do I fail and to no avail,
When I want to be glad and free.
The load drags me down and I nearly drown,
Weak and frail, in a troubled sea.

When I reach journey's end and the trials are o'er
And I see you, God's own dear Son,
Bear me safely o'er, to Your golden shore
And I pray Thou wilt say, 'Well done.'

Winifred R Pettitt

THE WRONG TROUSERS

I eyed the cupboard with wistful stare,
At the rows of trousers hanging there,
For two years inviting the discerning taste,
That crisp new material - oh what a waste (waist).

Last winter I resolved to lessen my girth,
A subject to bring out my dear wife's mirth!
Put off to the spring, then summer had gone,
My intention's melted - could it be the sun?

As autumn came, I wouldn't be beat,
Get into those strides and start to look neat,
I surely wouldn't let my honest intents
Be defeated by some more expense!

Well - here comes the New Year - back to square one
Fresh challenges have just begun,
Surely this time I won't keep quiet,
I'll fight the flab and beat the diet!

I open the wardrobe and pull in my tum,
The time of reckoning has come!
But wait - wasn't that my dinner call?
There's dumplings, thick gravy, cream puddings
and all,

Help!

Brian Fisher

WALKING IN THE PARK

As I was walking in the park
The children were playing and the dog gave a bark
The ducks were swimming upon the lake
What a beautiful day our Lord did make
Two old ladies sitting on a seat
Eating an ice-cream, oh what a treat
The beautiful gardens all in bloom
The birds are singing, all in tune,
My aching back, my tired feet
I think I'll have to find a seat
I sat and watched the world go by
Took a deep breath and gave a big sigh
I closed my eyes to have a short nap
When I felt on my shoulder a little tap
Excuse me madam it's time to go
The gates must be locked it's sad I know
So off I went on my way home
Tomorrow I'll bring the dog a bone
And when I go to sleep tonight
I'll think of tomorrow and all things bright

Elizabeth Ann Holt

RELIGION AND CIVILIZATION

Whether you believe in God or not
If religion fades, then so does civilization.
These few words you can be sure,
Are worthy of consideration.

For who made the sun the moon and the stars,
All the galaxies from Pluto to Mars?
Many inventions man can make,
But living creatures, only God can create.

He sent His only Son to Earth,
And gave Him such a lowly birth.
He came to teach us to live each day,
Together in perfect harmony.

So if we follow the rules He has made,
And listen to his voice, when He has said,
Love one another, as I have loved you,
The whole world will be better, I'm sure that is true.

So if you are filled with trouble and strife,
You find yourself thinking of another life.
You find yourself saying a little prayer,
Hoping that God is really there.

Someone to help when the going gets rough,
Someone to talk to when life is tough.
Someone to give you the strength that you need,
One who is a true friend indeed.

Iris Covell

ROSES FROM SOMEONE I LOVE

I woke in the night and saw them there,
Beautiful pink roses ever so fair.
They stood up so proud,
Their heads held high.
Looking at me on a table by my side.
It was twilight on the ward,
But what did it matter.
Those pink roses were there from someone I love.
I went back to sleep with a warm glow inside me.
I'll wake in the morning
They'll still be beside me.

Marion Lee

THE MORNINGS

I wake, sensing somehow that you're there
Lying so close beside me, gently sleeping
My nose, unsullied by tobacco welcomes
The warm morning scent of hair and skin
My eyes, now accustomed to the early light
Can once again lovingly caress your body
I'll never have too much of looking at you
To see you lying there, back towards me
I thrill again at your pillow spread red hair
Lightly tanned skin on arms and neck joins
That slender back sweeping nipped to hips
Those glorious dimples denting your cheeks
Long legs stretching far down by my own
To touch, to kiss, to taste, to drown within
Would make it all seem like heaven again
On some other days I've been that selfish
But now I'll just drink all of your beauty in.
And savour the pleasure of these moments
So I'll not forget this perfect, precious sight
Now my mind, becoming aware of the day
Screams loudly at me to once again accept
That I'm really lying here on my own, and yes
This tear worn face of mine must sadly rise
To meet another lonely morning without you.

Bob Newell

TO SOMEONE SPECIAL

You mean something very special to me,
When you are around,
You make me feel very glad,
You give me the confidence to carry on
Even when I do not feel very strong,
Especially when everything seems to be
Going wrong.

Just knowing that you care,
Also that you will always be there
Helps me through those difficult times
Knowing also that you are willing to share
The love that grows stronger every year.

Sometimes I can be difficult, that much is true
But deep down, I really do care for you,
You are my pride and joy
My dream come true
My one and only
That much I have to say
Also that I love you more each day

So let our love glow for all to see
And then you may realise that I really
Am in love with thee . . .

Mary Jones

LAST CONVOY

I came home in September with all the voyage done
To meet those well remembered and hear the talk of town,
To dare the season's weather and drink the deep brown ale
That sings the songs of evening and tells a roving tale.

And early in October when all the leaves came down
I waited for the lucky lads that brought the laggards home:
But this one and the other that friended me so sure
Live laughing of a morning, had quickly gone before.

So, lately in November when all the earth was brown
The lees of land were left me and soon the sun was gone,
And there were none to know me and there were none to find
But empty seats in bar-rooms and girls who could not mind:

At last in dead December I took the road I knew
Home haven lightly leaving where my concerning grew -
For land horizons beckon but sea horizon's known -
A question and an answer for one man alone.

Leonard Fifield

ABSENT FRIENDS

Drink a toast to absent friends
Blessings that the friendship sends
Enduring parting through the years
Sharing through laughter and tears

Raise your glass to the empty chair
The friend who should be sitting there
Bless you friend, though we're apart
I cherish your friendship in my heart

With the wine we celebrate
Friendships brought to us by fate
Through the years as friendships grow
Cheers to the friends we are proud to know

B Eyre

WHO?

Our gaze fell upon an autumn sky
And a sight which never before had met out eyes.
Blazing light all reds and greens.
A flaming object shimmered and gleamed.
We were spellbound unmoving from that eerie sight
Nor reason no cause could we procure
Did it really happen?
Will we ever know for sure?

C Collins-Reed

BELOW A SEA OF PASSION BEYOND . . .

Below a sea of passion
Beyond the coral reef,
On a bed of broken promises
Foolish hearts have come to grief.

So harken to me before you tread
Into this ocean of life,
For coral may be charming,
But will slash you like a knife.

Now I have swam these tranquil waters
In a bay of pink champagne,
But just below the rippled surface,
Riptides wait to claim.

Love is a pearl from an oyster
With a bloom of radiant pink,
Sadly, it changes in a second,
Forever scuttled in the drink.

So if you must venture out
Beyond the waters safe,
Be sure in swimming, you are strong!
. . . Or meet a mariner's grave.

Peter Mitchell McCulloch

A FAITHFUL FRIEND

When I was young, I had a friend,
I loved with all my heart.
But in my youth and ignorance
thought we would never part.

For many years we walked around
and gaily played together.
We'd run along the sandy beach
or stroll among the heather.

My parents knew my love for him,
and said he was a treasure.
To me - he was my whole wide world,
I loved him beyond measure.

But, as time went by, I realized
that he was not too well.
My dear, dear friend was slowing down,
and once or twice he fell.

One day, I woke - and he was gone
- my faithful loving hound.
No longer would I hear him bark
or see him running round.

But, I will ne'er forget my friend
- he meant the world to me,
and so he'll always have a place
in my heart and memory.

Joyce M Baker

GOD'S GIFT

That clenched fist of a rose bud,
looks threatening in the wind,
till gently God unwraps the spring -
His peace in healing rivulets -
and fresh hope spreads wherever life begins.

The flower feels for ears aware
of something yearning for this cheering change
and soon we see the first results
as petals shyly stretch to taste the breeze
until a mighty plan unfolds: a brilliantly mature

and complex bloom reveals its head,
a ruby in Creation's massive brooch,
a picture of the people
who will yield hurt selves to God -
He will touch them with His radiance and love.

Peter Comaish

WHAT IS LOVE?

Love is the greatest mystery of all,
With feeling undefined yet set so strong,
That naught can break the bond however long,
The time or distance separates the call;
But what nature forms the base of this enthral,
This chaining where you feel that you belong,
With the beloved where you sing the song,
In a unity and link of the shared fall.

But love is far more mixed with pain than joy,
Where anguish far exceeds all sense of bliss,
That the spirit finds no comfort in its lie,
Although your heart would beg this with a sigh,
Would hold that instant peak when you both kiss,
Yet all the rest is bound in turmoiled cloy.

Aileen Hopkins

DANCE AS ONE

Come closer lover
let me hold you, whisper in your ear
I love you
I'll say it softly, only you will hear

O how your scent smells like the rose in bloom
on a summer's day
O how your hair shines like the harvest moon
on a cloudless night

Come nearer lover
let me wrap my arms around your waist
I love you
pull you to me in a lover's embrace

O how your eyes sparkle like the diamonds on a ring
worn upon your finger
O how your voice sighs like the beating of a wing
upon an angel's back

Come dear lover
let us dance as one this night together
I love you
and we both will make it last forever

A J Evans

ELUSIVE LOVE

Misery's child lift up your head,
Flowers of hope they are not dead.
What if love has let you down,
And your dreams in fetters bound.

There'll surely come another day,
When a love will come to stay.
Don't be afraid to let love in,
To love someone is not a sin.

You can't dwell in halls of night,
When the sun is shining bright.
And though your heart be full of pain,
The time to dream will come again.

So many dreams may come and go,
Leaving you in depths of woe.
But the young can always rise,
With fresh stardust in their eyes.

The springtime of life is very sweet,
So every day with rapture greet.
It will do wonders for your dimples,
And may even cure your pimples.

Misery's child you've much to learn,
Love can leave your heart to yearn,
Can walk away and leave you lone,
When you think a love you own.

Too many roses have a thorn,
Many dreams should not be born.
And surely there will come a day,
When a love will come and stay.

Thomas Boyle

NEW YEAR RESOLUTIONS OR MISSION IMPOSSIBLE?

We make our resolutions now
The New Year has begun.
How long will we remember them
When all is said and done?

We'll try to be more kindly
When other folks we greet
And give them all a lovely smile
As in the street we meet.

We'll try to be more tolerant
Of other people's fears
And prove by our kind actions
That there is someone who cares.

We'll do our best to aid those
Who need a helping hand,
And in spite of much indifference
They'll know *we* understand.

We'll be a bit more generous
When asked to give again
To help sick or homeless people
Or ease someone else's pain.

In our little corner
Of this Planet Earth
Each one has a duty
To prove just what they're worth.

If we've failed our mission
When it comes to end of year
Our only consolation is -
Well the *thought* was there!

Mollie D Earl

EVENTIDE

Honeysuckle lanes to stroll
Entwined in love at eventide,
Distant farm dogs
Sound their warning,
While church bells call my soul.

Amelia Canning

WHEN THE SNOW CAME . . .

On a shivering star-filled night
A vision came to me
A girl whose beauty unsurpassed
Most men would never see.

I held her tightly in my arms
And gazed into her eyes
I did not feel the cold at all
Wrapped in her silken thighs.

But as our lust subsided
So my vision had to go
And when I woke the next morning
Love had melted with the snow.

Will she come again next snowy night
And will our bodies meet
Or shall I be left with an empty heart
And a damp patch on the sheet?

Tony J Cox

EYES OF EMOTION

Many a story can be told
      When eyes unfold
Eyes that sparkle with a greeting
      At one's first meeting
Eyes that show pain
      A frown is their frame
Eyes with sadness
      Wishing there was gladness
Eyes showing hunger
      Often just wonder
Eyes of fear
      Usually glare and stare
Eyes that are suspicious
      Are just as serious
When tears are in eyes
      It is happy or sad lives
Eyes when angry or cross
      Caused by a friend or your boss
Smiling eyes show laughter
      Which is what we are all after
Many a feeling can be bold
      With these eyes I am told

Susan Gerry

COLOURS OF LIFE

Golden yellow as the morning sun,
Orange red when the day has run.
Grass so green in its vernal dress
But dull and faded after summer stress.

All colours change with time we see
Like everything in life, and so do we.
Black-haired beauties turn to grey
So too blondes when they've had their day.

We can't do anything to halt the flight of time
Everything changes once we start to climb
The ladder of life, and it affects us all
Until that day when we get our call.

The call that comes at the end of our day
Has to be answered in the only way
That we know how, so we make our peace
As our colour changes when we decease.

Gerard Oxley

START WITH A SMILE

You laugh, and the world will laugh with you.
Yet cry, and you'll cry all alone.
Some laughter each day
keeps the doctor at bay,
'tis the best medicine that is known.

Although life may now be a struggle
and laughter seems so far away.
It's all up to you
how you will win through.
Be determined - you'll get there one day.

So start with a smile every morning
and people will smile back at you.
You'll find very soon
your world's back 'in tune'
and you'll wonder why you felt so 'blue'.

Joan Zambelli

TEDDY BEAR

Favourite toy of childhood
The wonderful teddy bear,
Pooh throwing sticks in the river,
Paddington taking the train.
Rupert and pals on adventure
Solving mystery along leafy lane.
Tiny Titanic Ted once belonged
To chief of that ill-fated ship.
In many a childish diary,
Teddy is there on each page,
Comforter, confidante, friend.
Tucked away in memory,
Warmly hugged, love by tots,
From generation to generation.
There's a lot to be said for Teddy
Contributory to a happy home.

Freda Grieve

A RAY OF HOPE

To care for others
Is a gift that's blessed
In a world so full of hatred, bitterness
To shine a light
A ray of hope
To those whose lives
Now cannot cope
Must surely be a world apart
From those of us
Who have no heart
In a world
That shows no tenderness
To care for others
Is a gift that's blessed

Arthur Harvey

THE AGE OF THE CRIMINAL

We live today in such difficult times
Forever bewailing the increase in crimes
A prisoner in our own home, with locks and chain
I'm beginning to think this world is insane.

A helpless old lady is knocked to the ground
All for the sake of stealing a pound
Children are threatened and bullied in school
By moronic louts who think it's 'cool'

Blame poverty or drugs for crime in part
But what really matters is what's in one's heart
Like an animal hunting prey without remorse
So the criminal follows a similar course.

Inner city riots are quite commonplace
Why can't we live together, whatever our race
In peace and love, for God made us all
Where prejudice exists, there stands a brick wall.

To the miscreant goes out this appeal
Try to imagine how the victim must feel
Or what hope do we have in this world full of sadness
For everything, everything, yes everything's madness.

Jeanne Ellmore

A FIGHT FOR LIFE

There are so many hard times
A cancer sufferer must endure
Is there light at the end of the tunnel?
Or how about a cure?
We are not sure why this happens
But it's an agonising time
We suffer more than prisoners
And they're guilty of a crime
Some have supportive families
But alas some have not
We wish for health and happiness
Why can't we have the lot?
We have many doctors and scientists
Working hard all day
Trying so hard to find a cure
Fingers crossed it's on its way
Research is so expensive
So please give what you can afford
Never lose your hope for life
Don't sit there being bored
Women of the world united
Please don't forget to fight
Keep on thinking positive
Always looking for that light

Catherine Halliburton

THE HORSE CHESTNUT TREE

I'm a magnificent horse chestnut tree,
In spring a wondrous sight to see.
My blossoms like candles in the sky,
Give pleasure to all who pass me by.

In summer with its warming sun,
The formation of my fruit's begun.
My leaves take on a darker shade,
A cooling shelter they have made.

Autumn is the time I fear,
It's a bad time for me each year.
Boys with sticks my body beat,
To knock down fruit they cannot eat

When winter comes my frame is bare,
With bruises and scratches everywhere.
Along comes spring to ease my pain,
Then the cycle must start again.

Mick Moyce

A LIFETIME

Some things only come with age
When you know you're turning your last page,
Of a life so precious
You took for granted,
Now you look back
At the things you've mantled,
The things you put off until tomorrow
While handling the happiness
The love and the sorrow,
Before you know it
The years have flown,
You're getting old
Your kids are up and grown,
Where's time gone?
What's it all been for?
Is this our only life
Or is there more?
Thoughts remain inside of me
We only live once
Or do we?

Joan Farlow

AGAIN

It's way after midnight and I should be sleeping
but I can't because you're not here.
Private thoughts in my head I am keeping
and in my solitude I shed a silent tear.
Never knew before I could feel this way,
never knew love could cause such pain.
I miss the man, the voice, the smile,
and want to hold him in my arms again, again and again.
I remember the first time I saw you,
your eyes looked right into my soul.
You smiled at me, you said hello
and gently my heart you stole.
I never even felt you take it,
never missed it when I was with you,
but now without reason you're silent and invisible
and my heart can't find its way home.
It's way after midnight and I should be sleeping
but I can't because you're not here.
I miss the man, the voice, the smile
and want to hold him in my arms again, again and again.

Gez Larkin

ANOMALIES

Such massive sums being spent
On probing into space
While half the world is starving
Homelessness grows apace

More roads, more cars, less countryside
To seek for leisure days
Videos, computers, Internet, et al
Make less work in many ways

With our modern medicine
Lots of disease wiped out
But AIDS is spreading, other ills
Will come along, no doubt

So many sad abortions
Others who wait and long
For a child to call their own
Something here seems so wrong

Drugs, crime, fat cats in the news
Yet we must not despair
Many strive to put things right
Always, there's those who care.

D Dosson

MY NEED

I need a lover of my kind of music, rock ballads of old,
I need a lover to share my beauty of colours pale and bold
I need a lover to tune into my moody blues
I need a lover of laughter and quick wit,
I need a lover to understand my anger when in a fit
I need a lover to counsel me when in doubt,
I need a lover who is loath to shout
I need a lover who shares my oneness with animals
I need a lover whose energy he's prepared to channel
Down avenue of tall vociferous tendril-hanging trees
In horror of nightmares leaving me shaking in a freeze
Most of all, I need a lover.

Jay Baker

TOGETHER, FOREVER, NO MORE
NEVER FORGET AS WE DEPART

A cry in the wind,
Is never lost.
The love forgotten,
Is always near.
Two lost souls,
Will be together.
Hand in hand,
We love each other.
Eye to eye,
We see each other.
Slowly, slowly,
We move together.
Only you can see me now.
Your eyes so clear,
I see before me,
And always a tear
For me you cry.
Paint a picture
Of days gone by.
Of endless days,
To sunset beaches,
Through sleepless nights,
Remember me,
As I remember you,
No more we are,
            Together.

Craig Alan Hornby

THE EYES OF FAITH

I see Him in the beauty of the flowers
I see Him in the rain and gentle showers
I see Him in the unfolding of a lovely rose
And feel His touch at the quiet close
Of the day, my soul in calm repose
I see Him in the radiance of the sunset
And the splendour of the dawn
And give Him thanks for every morn
My eyes He wills to see
I see His miracle of life, in every child that's born
And bless Him for the life He gives to me
I see His glory in the lustre of the stars
His handiwork in every activity of sky
The blazing of the sun in outer space, his power
Proclaiming God, and as the clouds roll by
Overhead, I lift my heart to Him in wordless praise
I see Him in the dark of the night
And in the light of day
I find Him in the merry month of May
And sense His nearness in December's grey
I see His grandeur in the outline of the mountains
His power in the lashing and the fury of the sea
I see Him in every great act of love
Wherever there is pity
I see Him in the animals and every form of life
On earth, and in every noble sacrifice
That man embraces for his brother   .
And His tenderness in the devotion of a mother
But on the Cross of Jesus I see a love
Which is greater than all other.

M D Walshe

RAILWAY JOURNEY

Silently waiting for the train
Watching the platform clock.
Ready to start our journey
into the train we flock.
Goodbye to the railway architecture
farewell to the bustling towns.
Whizzing along through tunnels
changing countryside abounds.
Gazing through misty windows
peering at far off hills.
Past rows of dappled fields
pale sunshine spills.
See the painted cottages
nestling amongst the trees.
Peeping over shaggy hedges
banks of wild flowers please.
Sudden flashes of bright colour
many crimson poppies grow.
Making a brilliant carpet
in green fields below.
Sunlight sparkles on sea water
as we are hugging the coast.
Reaching on the white cliffs
and all the passing boats.
Arriving at the station
the busy guard shouts.
Having reached our destination
we gather up our coats.

Joan Hawkes

IF I SHOULD LOSE YOUR LOVE

If I should ever lose the love
That lies deep within my breast
If I should ever lose that love
I could no longer rest

If I should ever lose the love
You to me did freely give
If I should ever lose that love
No longer would I live

My world would in darkness lie
For all eternity
If I should ever lose that love
That love you gave to me.

Gilbert H Waudby

NOT FOR ME

As my grandchildren say 'Nan it is so easy'
I'm thinking living in the nineties is no good for me
For I have only just mastered the calculator
And still I dare not use my coffee percolator
As I watch my grandchildren using their computers
I realise I would need at least a dozen tutors.
So I switch on the tele and the news it brings
And wonder who these people are doing these sick things
All these dreadful stabbing and in broad daylight
No longer dare I walk out alone at night
Abusing little children and their pets as well
I'm trying to remember when our standards fell
Hundreds made redundant and very short of cash
The roast remains a memory as it's back to bangers and mash
But some have really prospered of this I must agree
As I notice in their driveways not one car but two or three
Some have got two houses and a mobile phone
While others sit in squalor completely on their own
Will the years two thousand bring a change of heart?
No I do not think so unless we play our part.

Barbara Ramsey

SOME BETTERS SOME GETTERS

One thing in the nineties I find altered; is while many young folk are so
great.
There are another section who are different; they prefer a handout
from the state.
They tell you they *have* had offers made them, work they really would
enjoy to do.
But no meals or transport are provided, something that they *had*
looked forward to.
Employers never offered *me* some meal cash, or attempt to bring
me to work,
Sometimes I had to get up very early, not to do so would mean that
I'd shirk.
Meals I packed and took along there with me, if not then I'd very
hungry be.
I'd have lost employment very quickly, had I asked my boss if he'd
feed me.
Thing I find so strange is that the parents never let the youngsters
go without.
Always they have cans of pop and radios, which they listen to at a
loud shout.
Always life to them is just a big game, thinking mum or dad
will always give.
Yet if suddenly their parents vanished, how on earth do these
kids think they'd live?
Such a pity they aren't trained from childhood to be good hard
working folk
People then would gladly listen to them, knowing it was sense
each time they spoke.
In many ways the nineties have shown progress, people talk of love
instead of hate,
But to me the big fly in the ointment, are those preferring handouts
from the state.

Barbara Goode

OLD PALS

Of all the people I have met,
Along life's colourful way,
It's just those whose friendship lasts,
Who keep in touch today.

At infants' and at junior school, my first best friend
Is still a friend - from the past -
In spite of years and miles between -
We write and meet - it lasts!

At grammar school and into teens,
With another pal - who shared so much;
Even now - past middle age -
And miles between - we still keep in touch!

The first friend I ever worked with,
It's really good for me to say -
I became her bridesmaid -
And we still write to this day.

Through careers and transfers
We have all to move on -
Marriages may part us -
But old pals remain the same.

New friends we may make -
From one year to the next.
But those who stand the test of time
And absence, we still keep on our 'list'.

Like family members - where
There is a bond so strong;
No distance or time can separate
Kindred spirits - together belong.

Dorothy G Limbert

CHRISTMAS GREETINGS TO MY LOVE

You are far away from Scotland the country of your birth,
Where the purple heathered mountains are the fairest on God's earth,
Where the rivers and the trout streams and the winding tinkling burns
Make the sweetest of sweet music when the wanderer returns,

You are far away from England where a lassie waits for you,
Though her heart is often heavy still her love is strong and true.
For the meadows and the moorlands have no beauty now you're gone,
The stars have lost their lustre and of birdsong there is none.

Though she loves her country dearly one thing I know is true,
She'd leave it all behind to be in Aussie, lad, with you,
Celebrating Christmas in the good old fashioned way,
With hearth and home and family on this our Lord's Birthday.

Blanche Marsden

THE PARTING

I knew this moment had to arrive,
I knew this day must dawn,
And I had to be strong to survive
The trauma of this morn.
In my mind I've gone over it all;
You stood in stark relief
Against the light . . . I looked appalled,
Brimming with disbelief.
My eyes pricked and smarted and, blinking
The tell-tale tears away,
I stood my ground firm without shrinking,
But fool heart did betray.
It pounded in my chest and throat,
I thought that you must hear.
Sweet peace and tranquillity I sought,
But all is lost a I fear.
The tears well and cascade down my cheek
Like a huge dam unstopp'd.
I had not wanted to appear weak,
But my facade I'd dropp'd.
I had intended to be so brave,
To smile with empathy,
But needs I find me a small dark cave
To hide from sympathy.

Gwendoline J Douglas

SNOWBOUND

Just for a moment, confusion
In the driving snow I saw her face,
My mind once more in turmoil,
It's love, I rest my case.
Snowfall, however heavy, will
In time, just fade away.
But love, however hopeless,
With me will always stay.
The raging storm now eases,
Though the heartache lingers on.
Making footprints in the virgin snow,
- How could I be so wrong?
Friendship I must settle for,
Our storm starts once again.
My thoughts of her so very warm,
That snow now turns to rain.
One thing I know for certain
As the sun is in the sky,
Our caring sharing friendship
I will treasure till I die!

Terence Bloodworth

SPIRIT OF WONDER

The wind blows strong upon the trees,
The rustling leaves, of brown and gold,
Lie crisp and dry, as I walk along,
The colours dazzle the eyes, and refresh the soul.
We are so small, in a world gone mad,
That the beauty of life, escapes us and that is sad,
A blossoming tree, a tiny flower,
That shows us of God's awesome power,
The light, that's edged on wings of flight,
Of birds, of every colour and hue,
Are all reflections, of God's love for you,
The wonderful skies, both blue and grey
All, have their place, in every day,
Oh! That the world, but pause - and wonder,
All good things, that come from above,
Are given with His perfect love.

Rita Hillier

DAVE KILNER AND THE POLO MINTS

Dave Kilner bought some Polo mints
They're his favourites as everyone knows
But when he opened the packet
The mints didn't have any holes
'I wonder where the holes are?' he cried
'This really is the pits'
For although he liked the outside parts
The holes were his favourite bits
He looked over there and he looked over here
And he looked everywhere around
He even looked where he could not see
But the holes were not to be found
'I'm not having this' he said to himself
And back into the shop went he
'These mints have got no holes in' he yelled
'And that's no good to me'
The shopkeeper smiled as they always do
When a customer starts to moan
'I'm sorry sir' he said to Dave
'But you can now buy the holes on their own'
So he handed Dave a packet of holes
Which he slipped into his jacket
And when he got outside the shop
He gingerly opened the packet
He thought they tasted exceedingly good
And in no time the holes were all gone
'Polo mints may be my favourites' he said
'But I'm going to buy the holes from now on'

Coleen Bradshaw

THE RIVER IN SPATE

I stood beside the swollen river,
watching as it swirled round stones,
creating a mini-waterfall
at each interruption. Then on again,
forever downwards, scenting the sea,
hearing that vast amount of water, call.

The branches, broken from the trees
by the storm, career madly about
like small boats. The webbed feet
of numerous ducks, paddle frantically
to prevent them being swept away -
then seek sanctuary in the nearby leat.

The river, which is usually so quiet
and calm, has suddenly gone mad!
The homes of countless small creatures
along its banks seem threatened -
what a precarious life is theirs,
in which mayhem and danger features!

Where does all the water come from?
Starting as it does from one small source
upstream, the river gains momentum,
draining the surrounding land as it goes.
The snows of winter, the torrential rain
add to its appetite whene'er they come.

But - come here in summertime
and a different story - all is so serene -
the ducks lazily, floating round and round -
the wavelets rippling quietly by.
The stones stand out, like guardians -
and all is peace - there's not a sound.

Joyce Hockley

THE 90'S

World leaders say, 'I am the best.'
Listen to them! Ignore these pests !
Politics put us in a mess
Just like being in the recess . . .

Bloodshed around the Earth
Ridding of innocent souls
Death overrules birth
Aiming for useless goals

Red alert! Global warming!
The sea is slowly rising!
This is one last warning!
In the 90's, what will become of the living?

Jenny Cheung

ATTIC ROOM

I watch the clouds race overhead
And, lone, I muse, upon my bed,
About the lady whom I love,
My gentle friend, my peaceful dove.
I ponder her spirit, her nature, her form;
I crave her presence; I long to adorn her
With fine treasures, robes of silk, the scent of orchids,
And shower the milk of human kindness at her feet.

Though I know that I shall never meet
These expectations, except just one,
And that to love until the sun forgets to rise
And greet my face; 'tis a love that warms this icy place,
That is my home away from home,
A place that leaves me feeling lone and loveless,
If not for the love, that surely came from heaven above;
A love so vibrant, true and strong;
Love such as this could never be wrong.

Still, the clouds race overhead,
And I remain here on my bed,
And yet I feel some joy inside,
Remembering that I need not hide my feelings
From the heavens above;
The moon and stars know of my love,
The wind and rain can read my thoughts,
And if my efforts came to nought,
They were not wasted; my love was true,
And more than that, it embraced you.

Graham Ronald Bell

COPING WITH LOSS

I know how it feels to be lonely
'Merry Christmas' to wish to myself
'Happy New Year' is to me only
Another year sat on the shelf.
The last waltz - my partner is missing,
I sit at the table and dream
He's again by my side and we're kissing
And dancing again as a team.
I tell my old friends that I'm leaving
My taxi has come to collect,
I don't let them see I am grieving
They say I must come to the next.
'A holiday is just what is needed'
Are words just to prove they don't know,
'Start a new life' is well heeded
But where, on my own, do I go?
If you've read the above and repeat it
For it's starting to happen to you,
Well - after a struggle I beat it
And although it's not easy to do
Take my advice and start fighting
With hobbies and pastimes galore
They're not idle words that I'm writing
I worked hard to even the score
New friends will soon tire of your grieving
This facet of life you must close
Make the effort, new life is believing
This rhyme is from someone who knows.

Pam Owers

ONE RESOLUTION

Do we make any resolutions
At the start of each new year?
Do we think that this institution's
A way to make our path clear?

Strange how we need a new beginning,
To clear the score sheet once more.
Clutching at straws to ways more winning,
Swimming weakly for the shore.

We should never discard experience,
Let's never forget the pain.
There is a need to keep remembrance,
Lest we might falter again!

Cherish also the good experience,
Which is worth its weight in gold.
Repeat it at every convenience,
There is value in things old!

We all enter each year with baggage,
A mixture of bad and good!
'Be selective' should be our adage,
Discard the bad if we could!

There is a whole new year just waiting
To be used by you and me.
Wasting it can be devastating!
Please use it all, full and free.

But just stop and think before you start!
Have you got Christ in your scene?
He is the Lord! Just give Him your heart!
Have the greatest year that's been!

Terry Bowen

TO LOVE IS TO SERVE

Yes, to love is to serve,
This I firmly believe;
A mother for her child
No effort will relieve.
A wife for her husband,
A husband for his wife,
Just serving the other
Gives purpose to each life.
As a gardener toils in love,
His labours kissed with rain,
Without joy in service,
Endearing words are vain.
So true love will blossom
Strengthening cords of love,
Imparting contentment
And peace from God above.
Because God loved us first
And through His precious Son,
The supreme sacrifice
For us, the victory won.
Jesus showed us the way,
His love to imitate,
Serving too, our neighbours,
No task will be too great.
So to love is to serve,
Not a bind or a chore,
But a joy and delight
And His truth to explore.

Janet Bowen

TRUE LOVE

The day is dull the weather drear,
As down my face there runs a tear.
I feel so sad, so low, bereft,
Because today my darling left.
Then suddenly there comes a shaft
Of sunlight through the gloom,
That lights not just the dreary day
But helps a hope to bloom.
My darling has not gone for good
I know he will be back.
I let a smile light up my face
And dry the teardrop's track.
With love like ours to fill the days
The time will soon fly past,
My darling will be home again
And out my gloom will cast.
For love like ours there is no end
It stretches through the years,
Will pass through even death's dark veil
Till Heaven's door appears.
I will not cry or feel depressed
For love will light the way
Until my darling one returns
And ever more will stay.

Winifred Jenkins

AUTUMN

The wind is in a hurry
As it rushes 'thro the trees
And leaves of brown and yellow
Are dancing in the breeze.

They whirl and twirl and pirouette
Then settle on the ground,
To make a magic carpet
Of green and gold and brown.

The rustling autumn carpet
Whispering 'neath our feet
Is mirrored in the sunset,
To make our day complete.

Emma Hunt

TO MUM AND DAD WITH LOVE

A mum and dad with hearts of gold,
Hardworking, loving, always there,
You taught me those special ways
Happiness, sharing, how to care.
A kiss hello,
A kiss goodbye,
A loving hug if I should cry.
The memories of my childhood days
The Christmases of yesteryear
Such special times to me so dear.
If I could have chosen you myself
I wouldn't change a thing
No-one could ever hope to have
Such a special mum and dad.
I know I'm lucky
That's why I want to say
How much I love you both today
And always.

Bridget Ward

NO GUARANTEE

Sitting alone, dejected, rejected,
cursing and swearing - why me?
I think of the words of a friend who cares,
why not? - Life has no guarantee.

It's not how we planned it, this heartache and pain,
it's not what we want - but it's ours just the same.
Life is unfair no one can deny
that it deals cruel blows and we do not know why.

And it's really not true that time heals wounds,
the passing of time fades scars.
The wounds remain to remind us
of the value of who we are.

We must count our blessing, though they often seem few
we must soldier on in the things that we do.
Conquer each day - give thanks at the end
for some treasured second, or some treasured friend.

Search for the bright side, keep love in your heart
and hope that one day you'll find,
not the fortune or fame of great living,
but *acceptance* that brings peace of mind.

Audrey Woodall

GIVE ME PATIENCE LORD

Are our prayers being answered straight away?
Oh do we worry and get in a state?
Our dear Lord is never in a hurry,
Therefore we must be patient and wait.

Let us just give Him our time every day,
Knowing He's given us the best that He could.
For we must accept His Will and His way,
Then He'll give us whatever is good.

For He has the whole of Eternity
To do all the things that He wants to do
He'll do what He can, in His own good time,
Giving great blessings to me and to you.

Eunice C Squire

MY FAITHFUL FRIEND

Born to be a friend to me
Forever by my side
Together we have laughed and played
Our hearts were open wide

You're ever in my thoughts my friend
With your mischievous looks and ways
And I know that I will ne'er forget
You! Through all my days

You've comforted me when I was sad
Though you never spoke one word
You never once betrayed me
Of all the things you heard

You are always pleased to see me
With each new start of day
As you look at me with tender eyes
That have a wealth to say

As my friend you never ask too much
Just a titbit and a walk will do
And in return you give so much
My faithful friend are you.

John Lowe

THE JOURNEY

My body aches
I begin to weep
What's all this commotion
I just want to sleep

I open my eyes
The pain's now gone
A caring voice says
It won't be long.

My soul is lifted
I look back at the shell
Of what was once me
All is well

An ebony darkness
Engulfs my eyes
Then flashbacks and pictures
Of days gone by

I'm floating and moving
At the speed of light
I reach the destination
It's all alright

Embraced by the warmth
And wonderful rays
It's where I'm to spend
The rest of my days

I meet more people
We're no longer nervous
We all feel welcome
As He comes for us.

He takes my hand
Wide open eyes
Lovingly guides me
Towards paradise

So this is Heaven
What a lovely place
I would never return
To the pain-filled days.

Tracy Roberts

ONE FEBRUARY MORN

On a Cotswold hill one February morn
To a white faced ewe a lamb was born
It steamed in the chill of the first light of day
and the white face ewe licked as its life ebbed away
The grass was white from an iron frost
She could not comprehend that its small life was lost
When the shepherd arrived later that day
He picked up the lamb and led her away
She would stop and stamp on the hard frosted ground
Then look and listen for a trace of a sound
From her long lost lamb.
Back at the farm in a sweet smelling stall
She stood and called from her shelter of straw
While other ewes suckled their lambs
She was destined to call stamp and stand. Alone.
But as darkness fell the shepherd came back
His hurricane lamp throwing light through a crack in the door,
Which flooded across the stone flag floor as it opened wide
The ewe's ears pricked as a small lamb cried
From the shepherd's arms.
It had been his desire to put the lamb by the warm fire
Tended by his wife
And awakened the dying spark of the poor lamb's life.
The old ewe nuzzled as the young lamb suckled and wriggled its tail
The latch closed on the old barn door
And again darkness fell.

Roger Stokes

WHY

Why do people have to die
And leave you all alone
Change your life around completely
So your house is not a home

Make the memories you're left with
A painful haunting rhyme
Make you ponder whether living
Is some futile waste of time

Will the love I shared with you dear
Give me strength to live as one
Will the happiness we had here
Be my reason to go on

Janet Merola

A JOURNEY OF THE HEART

These emotions of love that swell inside, they're ebbing
      and flowing without calming, or pride.
One touch brings on groundswells to heights then unknown,
      they're wanting to think that love's seeds have been sown.
Being close raises passions, from deep deep within,
      love's emotional arrows are about to begin.
Stop now, or go forward, the decision to make,
Now with youth comes this time of pain and heartache.
Each beautiful meeting stirs feelings the same, when learning
      the rules of love's emotional game.
Searching love's misty pathways is so, so sublime, where there
      is no reason, nor any rhyme.
This road to discovery, is wavering, and long, to the home
      where you'll find, your love does belong.
Then comes a chance meeting, where vibrations are one,
      and the whole wondrous cycle again has begun.
When your way has been found, and fulfilment is near,
      the end of love's journey, is ever so dear.

Alan Smith

THEN THERE'S YOU
(For James)

I sometimes become disillusioned
Sometimes a little fed-up
Sometimes I don't seem to be getting anywhere
And I just feel like giving up,
But then there's you.

When life gets on top of me
And I lose the will to fight
And I slip into despair
As nothing seems to be right,
Then there's you.

When everything I plan
Seems to go wrong
When I feel lonely
And can't seem to find a place to belong,
Then there's you.

Then there's you,
Even when I just need someone to listen
Or someone to listen to
When I just need a hug, a squeeze or a smile
Then there's you.

Karen S Parsons

A CAUTIONARY TALE

'Now be careful it's diluted acid you use,'
The students were sternly warned.
'You don't want to cause an explosion
When your chemical solution is warmed.'

Now Helena was known to be naughty,
And never obeyed what was said,
So when she was told 'Use diluted,'
She used concentrated instead!

The test-tube hung over the burner,
Absorbing the heat with greed.
Whilst Helena stood there in a day-dream,
The acid reacted with speed.

There suddenly came an explosion,
And Helena was blown out of view,
Complete with test-tube and burner,
And brand new laboratory too!

Though they never did find poor Helena,
A conclusion they certainly had -
'Method' - use the wrong type of acid,
'Result' - lost, one girl and a lab.

Geraldine Foy

THE SNOWMAN WHO CAME BACK

Little Suki loved the snowman
With buttons for eyes and a smart bow tie
His hat at a jaunty angle
On the lawn with spirits high
He wore a scarf to keep out the cold
And a pipe for comfort I'm told

Little Suki called him Snowy
Well, he did prove a little showy
But the thaw took away poor Snowy
There was only a heap of wet snow
With a scarf, hat, pipe and bow
And little Suki was unhappy and sad

But the rolling year grew old
And winter returned with icy cold
It snowed all night and at the dawn
There was Snowy in the middle of the lawn
Across the garden, there was the track
Of dear old Snowy who did come back.

Will Amos

PROMISES KEPT

Promises kept,
E'en as I wept,
His face looked into mine,
What peace and love,
Showered from above,
From Our Father so divine.

Holding my hand,
Please understand,
His voice so soft and kind,
All will be well,
The truth I tell,
His words assuaged my mind.

Keeping me strong,
All the day long,
Right into anxious night,
Feeling his arms,
Powerful yet calm,
Fear not my child - hold tight!

Mary Wheatley

TWO NAMELESS SPIRITS

Two nameless spirits on the Dun heath
Smile and greet, but do not touch.
And joy shines through them -
The light-grey mists part and swirl;
Little tinted birds dart and sing . . .
Bees hum; animals stir
Because of Them!
These two lovers who have
Endless time without pain -
The dark ground throbs: at their being,
The seconds as they were: of
Human-kind. Crystal joy,
Sweet ecstasy -
As she says 'Farewell' to him;
Enfolds the two, to Blackness.
Night on the heath returns.
And Nature had known such delight
Twisted and writhed in gladness
Because of Them!
Two nameless Spirits.

L P B

OUR GOD CREATED EVERYTHING

There's so much beauty in everything
If we look around and see
A flower when it opens its petals
The curving branch on a tree.

Many are the blessings that
The Lord God has given us
Taking time to look around
At everything so plenteous.

The gracefulness of seagulls in flight
With silver wings out spread
Wheeling and swooping round about
Hungry, looking to be fed.

The sea with exotic coloured fish
Mysterious as they swish and twist
Enjoying their freedom swimming around
In the vastness where they exist

So much beauty created in love
God's wonderful goodness and grace
He's always been there to care
Providing for all the human race.

Dorothy Price

STICKS

There came a guy from out of the sticks
Regarded as a hick by the city slicks.
But being educated physical and bright
With brain or brawn he could win a fight.

In no way was he any sort of duff
And clearly made of the sterner stuff.
With a sound broadly-based background
Which in our leaders is seldom found.

He came across many of the Oxbridge crew
Outshining them all bar a few.
Whether in business or in the bar
It was he who invariably was the star.

Whether working the city or in the sticks
He used his abilities and all his tricks.
To forge such an outstanding professional career
Before too long he had no peer.

By using his brains he has made a mint
Never in life will he be skint.
His worth eloquence and outstanding charms
Took him to more than the ladies' arms.

In every arena his skills were applied
Till he chose a woman really satisfied.
And now he's got a wealthy wife
And returned contented to country life.

James Young

A POIGNANT THOUGHT AS ONE'S BODY GROWS OLD

Make age and ageing no concern of thine,
Life is but a brief encapsulation of your free spirit along
some unexplainable time line.
Your spirit hasn't weakened with the body's aged fragility,
It has grown ever more unique, serene, and understanding,
with each lesson of mortality.
It survived the incongruities, urgencies and trepidations of
youth, erstwhile,
And now it can reflect upon life's achievements and memories
with satisfaction and a wry smile.
When mortality is spent, onward your spirit will fly,
continuing along some other time line,
Ever learning, ever experiencing, until, at last, it becomes
complete, pure, unique and divine.

G E Khandelwal

EVENING HYMN

Sunset borrowing colours from Vulcan's store,
Delicately paling to pastels from the rainbow;
Silhouetting a leaf, firing wavelets on the shore,
Bright until, slowly dying, the flames will go.

Within the village church a thousand jewels glow,
The sun's last fingers search the old grey stone;
And chorusing birds hymn God's fiery show.
I find myself unmoved by this - alone.

The evening hymn chokes as light fades in the West,
A watery film clouds, I cannot see.
The East awakes as we turn to our rest -
And you are half a world away from me.

Di Bagshawe

THE NEW YEAR

As a new year is about to begin,
It usually starts with a happy grin.
New resolutions made with vigour;
Happy thoughts it does trigger.
We know most likely we will break,
All the resolves we made in haste,
But what fun at the start of the year,
Only we know it usually ends with a tear.
For in between we have our ups and downs;
Happy days and some leave us with a frown.
New lives come and some depart,
Bringing us joy also breaking our heart.
This is what life is all about;
On new year we like to shout out,
All the good things we wish for loved ones,
With good health and happiness comes.
But stop and think of those without,
And pray to God to help those about,
Who are less fortunate than us,
And bless them and give them a life to trust.

Valerie Marshall

SGT JACK BASKEYFIELD V C

On a cold winter's day in November,
a statue was unveiled at Festival Heights.
To a soldier whose gallantry we remember
an action at Arnhem, with his comrades he unites.

He died destroying two tanks single-handedly.
His dead comrades lay all about,
as he proceeded to take out more armoury.
Despite being badly wounded throughout.

Imagine his thoughts, as he man-handled the gun,
Revenge, or just being a soldier.
He was the one, his mother's son,
who worked for the Co-op as a butcher.

The 21 year old soldier from Burslem,
who served in Africa and Italy.
Was to fight his last battle at Arnhem,
At the bridgehead, rearguard of the soldiery.

Sgt Baskeyfield made his supreme stance.
With extraordinary selfless courage,
to prevent the enemy advance,
from a position of extreme advantage.

His statue stands proudly, fifteen feet high.
An inspiration to his regiment, surely.
Young people of the Potteries pass by,
and see their own 'action man' clearly.

Hundreds of veterans witnessed the unveiling,
Proudly displaying their medals.
Though the wind blew, and the hail was hailing.
They marched to the drums and cymbals.

Raymond Baggaley

A PATHWAY TO HEAVEN

Sometimes I sit here all alone
And start to wonder why
Everyone I grow to love
Always seem to die
It makes me feel so angry
As I never get to say
Goodbye, God bless, or thank you
Before they pass away
First I lost my brother-in-law
And then I lost my dad
Next I lost my husband's mum
And then my dog as well
Last year I lost my brother's wife
This year my husband's dad
Also aunts and uncles
Which made me feel so sad
In January 1996
My brother nearly died
And now I feel so pleased to add
Thank God that he survived
So if you have a partner
Husband or a friend
Make sure that if you argue
You put things right again
As when you get to Heaven then
You'll feel so pleased to see
At least your friends and family
Are happy as can be.

Merilyn Gulley

THE THOUGHT WAS THERE

We turn over new leaves year after year
And mean to stick to the promises made.
As the days turn to weeks, then months, it begins to wear.
The promises become more forgotten and to fade.

Diets are thrown to one side, too many delights,
With too many calories and oh! Too much to forego.
To stop being selfish, help others with all our might,
Until we are upset, 'put on' and made feel low.

We make promises to never be too busy to listen.
To advise, never be destructive but just to be there.
But work, hustling and bustling just glisten,
Making it difficult and hard to really care.

Visiting older relatives and friends living alone,
We vow to make time once a week to see.
Eventually it means to now and again a phone,
But never make time to take time out for tea.

We will definitely cut down on the cigs and the drink,
Sweets, buns, cakes, biscuits and all things wicked.
To make our bodies more healthy and put us in the pink,
Jogging and exercises to keep the weight licked.

Does anyone intend to really keep the new leaves turned,
Or are they just promises to laugh about and burn.

A Hall

BIRTHRIGHT

He slips into the world quietly, senses intact
He sucks greedily at a wizened empty breast
Where lack of food and water have put nature to the test.
He feels hard earth everything dry
Burned by the sun in a cloudless sky.
Hears bombs, guns, cries
The knell of death as someone dies,
Smells burning, rotting human flesh
In camps surrounded by fences of mesh.
Sees with eyes in a shrunken face
The suffering and death of the human race.
Thinks as he lays down and breathes his last,
I'm glad this thing called life is past
He slips out of the world
Still quietly
Still black.

Maureen Delaney

ABYSSINIAN QUEEN

(For Sultana Begum Hussein and Andy Selim)

Fair Queen, there, 'pon Abyssinian lake,
someday, wilt thou my true heart take?
Descended from noblest Amharic blood,
thy beauty and grace do my senses flood.

Thou reclinest 'pon an ancient throne,
swathed, dunelike, 'cross a desert blown,
scentfill'd by myrrh and oriental musk,
flawless skin the hue of African dusk.

'Pon my tongue thou dost like honey taste,
thy maidenly virtue to my mind is chaste,
sensuous lips that spout refined prose,
offer'd henceforth, like a Turkish rose.

Thy throat, 'tis garb'd in Etruscan gold,
radiant and rich like yon' sun so bold,
flaxen hair doth smell like freshen'd spring,
mantl'd with jewels and Babylonian rings.

A thousand flowers, 'bout thy feet are toss'd,
'pon thee my Queen, they are not lost,
'Tis true, thou art gracefully serene,
a spectacle, mine eyes have ne'er before seen.

Fair Queen, there 'pon Abyssinian lake,
pray one day, wilt thou my true heart take?
Methinks, alas, thou wilt a love lost be,
Since thou wouldst give not thyself to me.

David Brasier

TO A CHILD

Love is being:
with people who love you,
fathered on midnight shoulders,
mothered in warm embrace,
dandled on nursery rhymes,
dawdled to play with friends,
afforded a childhood,
protected by constancy,
assured of self worth,
aware of the other,
taught by patient teacher,
careful with tender minds,
allowed freedom to develop,
able to make mistakes and amends,
encouraged to fulfil potential,
supported through dreams and disasters,
nurtured with understanding,
love is being; there.

Shirley Johnson

INFORMATION

We hope you have enjoyed reading this book - and that you will continue to enjoy it in the coming years.

If you like reading and writing poetry drop us a line, or give us a call, and we'll send you a free information pack.

Write to :-
Arrival Press Information
1-2 Wainman Road
Woodston
Peterborough
PE2 7BU
(01733) 230762